The Art of

Prayer

It takes a humble man to pray

NE Ngoveni

NE Ngoveni

Dedication

*B*eing my very first book ever, I would love to dedicate this book to my biological mother. I was raised in a village in an environment of pain. I did not experience the full intensity of the pain in my family, I believe, because the Lord chose to shield me from it. Now that I'm fully matured in age and spirit, I now understand that my mother went through so much that would have been unbearable for a normal person.

She grew up without a mother and couldn't complete her schooling simply because she had to work for herself. She was the second child of her parents and, although her father was alive, he was one of those fathers that you can't rely on. The first born, her brother, was also one of those. Life got so tough for her until the time she got married to my father by the grace of God. They were happy for a time and had five children of which I was the second born and only son.

Due to circumstances of life my father took a second wife who had three girls. We thank the Lord for their lives. I grew up seeing my mother and Daddy fight like enemies. I didn't know it was wrong at the time. I saw her tolerating things that I wouldn't advise anyone to tolerate. I saw her surviving storms that were probably a meal of everyday life for her. I saw her being rejected by family, community and, in particular, the church.

We, her children, were the only thing she had in life and her desire was to see us living better lives than she had. She told me that her prayer was to see us grow closer to God, to know Him and to serve Him despite all the things the world offers. Such a mother is a blessing. I wouldn't trade her for anything.

Just when I thought God would change the situation in my family, Daddy disappeared without a trace. He left home on a Friday, as had become the norm, to be with another woman that was known at home as his newly acquired woman. As a family we thought he would return until we were alerted the following Thursday by his work place that he had not been seen at work. We looked all over for him using every avenue at our disposal without success. It is now twenty-seven years that my dad has been gone.

I saw my mother handle this without breaking. She had a peculiar practice that we did not understand as children of crying to an invisible man, if I may put it like that. When I asked her about it she told me she was talking to the Lord about our situation because, "My child, He's the only one we have." I honestly didn't understand then what she was talking about. She told me it was called prayer and that it was talking to God about everything. I answered, "Really? But I never heard Him answering back?" She dismissed my words saying I was too young to understand and I had to let it go.

She usually sang in tongues with the melody of "Mayenziwe Intando Yakho" (Let your will be done). Today I'm delighted to tell the world, through this book, that my mother was a prayer warrior and that we are still standing as a family as a result of her answered prayers. She prayed her heart out for our future. As I have grown to know the Lord better, I have realized that His hand has been upon me even when I did not know Him. I can confidently tell you that prayer works and that God answer prayers.

Mommy you have instilled in us the best of habits which is to pray in all circumstances of life. I, therefore, would like to let the world know that I dedicate this book to you. It is not because you are my biological mother, but simply because I have watched you praying without ceasing. I observed you crying before the Lord. I saw you surviving storms of life because of this tradition of prayer. The enemy couldn't reach us because of this thing called prayer. Now that I have understanding, I can easily tell the world that you are a winner in Christ the Lord. You survived all types of storms against your life through prayer and you deserve this honor. Glory to God! You might not have taken us to the best schools but you taught us what teachers out there could not teach us. If there's one thing that you gave as a legacy to us, it is the tradition of prayer.

My first book is dedicated to you to honour you for teaching me, through life experience, what it means to pray in all circumstances. Let the world know that NE Ngoveni is a result of your prayers that were made in tough times. You were always patient with me and believed in me as a child that was elected by God from a very early age. Such a mother cannot be found in any shop around the world. You must have been sent from above to be who you are. May the Lord richly bless you even in your old age. You are such a blessing.

This book is dedicated to my mother - **Martha Masingita Mabasa.**

Table of Contents

Foreword

*P*rayer is our greatest privilege as believers and unfortunately we also need to admit that it is also our greatest and constant failure. It is a great mystery that many people still struggle to comprehend, no matter how long they have been in the church. Yet, when we pray and God answers our prayers immediately, we get perplexed and wonder why God would ask us to pray when He already knows what will happen after we have prayed. This book, written by Apostle N.E Ngoveni presents answers to many questions that we have on issues of prayer. It brings about a clear understanding of prayer and its dynamics to mature Christians and to the newly converted as well.

We live in a very loud and busy world and it takes a lot of effort and energy to get someone's attention. Getting them to turn off the radio, put their phone down, shut down their computer, stop driving, and park their car by the roadside, is no small task. If you succeed at this and they give you their attention - you are privileged. It is, therefore, hard to fathom that - when we pray - our words reach the very throne of God. Your prayer here on earth works wonders that you cannot comprehend. It activates God's power in heaven, and "God's will is done on earth as it is in heaven."

What was the first thing that the disciples and the early church embarked on after our Lord Jesus Christ ascended to heaven? *They returned to Jerusalem...to an upper room" and "continued with one accord in prayer and supplication...."* (Acts 1:12-14). If the disciples who walked with our Master for years still saw prayer as an integral part of their lives then we should also take prayer seriously.

This book points out that prayer is not merely submitting our requests to God but entails the pursuing of a deeper relationship with Him. We know that He knows what we need before we ask, so our prayers and requests are an acknowledgement that we fully rely and depend upon Him. With pride, and great joy, I commend this book to you!

Pastor Lungile Divine Marhungane
(President; WAGH Movement, South Africa)

Endorsements

*A*postle NE Ngoveni; when you are with him you smell a godly odour. He is a blessed man who fears the Lord and adores Him so much. Prayer is his second nature, therefore, a book on prayer by this young general is a must have. I bless him and his wife for such an impact in the lives of many. May you be blessed and established more in prayer as you forge ahead in your Christian walk. May you experience great favor from both men and God for this production and many more!

Prayer. The definition of prayer is *"spiritual communication between two spiritual beings wherein one is the pursuer and the other the pursuant as they seek to find each other and work together thereafter in an established covenant."*

Prayer is the tool and instrument for establishing new platforms and strengthening old ones. Prayer is the art of intermediary engagement towards a noble goal where restoration and resuscitation occurs. It is a platform where solid foundations and victories are established!

The Art of Prayer is not for the schooled, intellects or the great. It is a given and ordained ordinance from glory land to all who aspire and desire to connect with their Maker and Master at a zonal level in a spiritual LTE network. If the church had to reinvent her operations down here, I would advocate for more prayer than anything else because of its volume and impact towards God and the creation. God only responds to prayer when He acts on behalf of the people. "If my people who are called..." Battles and wars are not won on pulpits or battlefields but in the closet. Nations, climates and politics can be rearranged and reordered behind closed doors when the church is kneeling at the altar seeking God's face and His intervention. A church or ministry that has prayerful leaders and members can always enjoy the presence of God without gimmicks and manipulations. If the altar is occupied by wailing people then the heavenly odour graces the temple and removes the grave stench far away from the resurrected. I firmly believe that true, spot-on prophecy is a result of intense and intentional prayer! As we read this book may we receive the grace of both prophetic prayer and intercessory prayer. May we heed the call to prayer and start praying! God bless you as you connect with the heartbeat of this great leader.

Prophet S M Kunene
(Senior Pastor; Bochim Christian Centre, South Africa)

I recommend Apostle NE Ngoveni's new book with tremendous enthusiasm to every believer. Apostle Ngoveni is a brilliant man of God who is a living example of what he is teaching in this great book.

He has proven himself to be hardworking, dedicated, and has displayed excellence in leadership. He has lived up to its standard and has pioneered a great work at Impact House Ministries. He is also a father to many sons in the ministry. In this book Apostle NE Ngoveni is dealing with biblical foundations when it comes to prayer.

Apostle NE Ngoveni has learned so many great truths through his many years of ministry. He is a sought after conference speaker with great insight of God's word - a man for this generation. He has been a true inspiration to many in this life. His wisdom and insight on the subject of prayer will inspire you as you follow Jesus Christ.

The Art Of Prayer will show you the way and provide a guide into the secret of prayer. Prayer is an art, and as such, must be learned. This is a book every believer needs to read and study in the times we are living in.

Bishop Marius Ndjavera
(Senior Pastor; Gospel Truth Ministries, Namibia)

From the very moment I met NE Ngoveni, to the time the Lord Himself called him to the ministry, I sensed strongly within me that he was a choice vessel of God - a man with a fine and well balanced intellect. From his youth Apostle NE has always portrayed an unclouded focus and perception. His firm and unshakable determination has taken him deeper in his relationship with God.

Today I am greatly honoured and imperatively thankful to God for this opportunity to endorse this great and life-transforming book on prayer.

This book is a priceless treasure for anyone who desires to put behind them a superficial prayer life.

Prayer is the bedrock of every major move of God in the life of a nation, a church or an individual. It is the very breath of a spiritual life. It is so simple that a child can utter it yet so profound that it requires a lifetime to learn.

I highly recommend this book on *The Art of Prayer*. May you discover the highest ministry one can ever render to God as Apostle Ngoveni reveals the secrets of this outward and upward flow with the Creator. Great work Apostle.

Josh Moyo
(President; Destiny Empowered Christian Church, Perth, Western Australia)

Since its first mention or inception, the word "art" has been in constant use since the 1800s to our millennial age. According to the Merriam

Webster Dictionary one definition of the word "art" is, "a skill [craft, technique, knack, facility, ability, know-how] at doing a specified thing, typically one acquired through practice." Spanning across the ages there has been constant communication displayed through scripture between God and man which is known as prayer. In prayer man - with depth - responds to God's call to His deep. Adam walked with God, Moses spoke with God as a man speaks to his own friend, and Elijah persisted in prayer for the rain to come. Solomon worshipped and fire came down from heaven, Daniel prayed for twenty-one days, and Prophetess Annah prayed till the manifestation of the promise of Christ. Jesus Christ (God in man) prayed even while on the cross. You and I should also pray. In this book we will learn how to talk with God on a personal level and how to deal with issues of life through the many forms of prayer available to us. In Joel 2:9-10 the weak are encouraged to say, "I am a warrior", or, "I am skilled."

Art is to apply yourself well - at the right time and place - to meet a specific need.

Apostle NE Ngoveni is a man given to prayer and sound teaching of the word of God, well studied, and rightly dividing the word of truth. Prayer is a definite art [skill, craft, technique, knack, facility, ability, know-how]. When done well it surely yields results and fruit for "the effectual fervent prayer [skill, craft, technique, knack, facility, ability, know-how] of a righteous man availeth much.

The art of prayer and worship are identical, parallel in action and both achieve the result of accessing the heart and mind of God and the revelation of mysteries (Jeremiah 33:3).

Whatever you practise for ten thousand hours (one year, one month and seven days) becomes a part of you. Why not practise the Art Of Prayer?

Jesse Priestly
(Director; Platinum Level Records, Zimbabwe)

If you need to see a change in your life, your health, your circumstances, your attitude, your spouse, your children, or your church, learn to integrate prayer and worship. There is a correlation between prayer and worship and both are done by man unto the Lord God Almighty.

Prayer and worship are exclusively reserved for the Lord and form the largest part of our Christian walk. Prayer is, in its element, another form of worship or, put in a better way, it is the highest form of worship.

It is important for us to understand the concept of prayer and worship as both of these are necessities for building our relationship with the Father. Prayer is a God-given privilege that allows us access into His presence and worship, on the same token, is revering God. Prayer is God's invitation to us and worship is how we respond to Him -

the manner in which we approach our heavenly Father.

It is critical for us to notice in the Bible, particularly in the New Testament, that everyone who came to the Lord Jesus to ask, plead or pray him to attend to a personal request either worshipped Him first like the leper man who came and knelt before Him (Matthew 8:1-2) and the synagogue ruler who fell at His feet and pleaded (Mark 5:22-23). Some started with prayer and later switched to worship like the Cannanite woman who, after much rejection by Jesus and His disciples, came and knelt before Him (Matthew 15:22-29). Some worshipped after their prayer was answered like the Samaritan leper who threw himself at Jesus' feet after being healed (Luke 17:11-19).

Prayer is the petition or thanksgiving we are lifting up to the Lord and worship is the attitude in which we do it. In prayer we bring our request to the Lord and in worship we affirm His ability to bring it to pass.

When Jesus taught His disciples how to pray both in Matthew 6 and in Luke 11, He did not teach them a recital. It was not about what to pray but how to pray. He said, *"This, then, is how should pray."* In the first line, "Our Father in heaven," we acknowledge the one to whom we are praying as our Father which supposes a relationship with Him, and the second line, "Hallowed be your name" addresses the worship element. We are magnifying and attributing greatness to His name. All this comes way before you ask for bread and forgiveness. Prayer and worship are the two sides of the same coin you can't do without.

In prayer we communicate our desires to the Father and in worship we offer back to Him the desires He communicated to us. Your prayers are incomplete without worship and you cannot truly worship without prayer.

Churchill Selatole
(Author of "Dear Worship Leader")

Christianity is not a funfair but a warfare. The implication of the trusted work of calvary makes the outcome of this warfare a done deal in the favor of the believer. We can only cash in on this predetermined outcome by faith through salvation hence peculiar activations are required to take delivery of the manifestations.

Consequently, prayer becomes imperative being one of the strongest weapons of war for the believer.

And he spake a parable unto them to this end
that men ought always to pray and not to faint
Luke 18:1

To speak low of prayer or to pray less is simply to grow weak faster.

Study the book of Luke very well. Jesus lived a life of prayer, meditation and study of God's Word. He taught this lifestyle to the early church and first apostles which is evident in the book of the Acts of the Apostles.

This book, "The Art of Prayer," buttresses these points and drives the point home for believers fighting for continuous victory on earth.

Prayer becomes interesting when it provides solutions. It is not enough to pray but very needful to get solutions to the purpose of praying. This book offers you infallible wisdom on how to go about it, therefore, get copies for yourself and for the brethren.

See you at the top!

Apostle Osilu Ikechukwu
(Head servant, Royal Gilgal International Evangelism Ministry; Overseer of Freedom Christian Centre, Lagos Nigeria)

Apostle Ngoveni is a man sent to this generation by God to awaken and provoke the church to take its rightful position. From the time I have known him and from our encounters with the grace upon his life during our conferences in Lusaka Zambia, he has a unique way of presenting the revelation of God's word in a way that anyone can understand. I am confident that his book on prayer will most certainly take one to a higher level of understanding about prayer which is the life line of every child of God.

Bishop Marion Musonda
(Overseer & Founder; Gospel Ministries International, Lusaka, Zambia)

Against The Spirit of Herod

Introduction

5 Peter therefore was kept in prison: but prayer was made without ceasing of the church unto God for him. 6 And when Herod would have brought him forth, the same night Peter was sleeping between two soldiers, bound with two chains: and the keepers before the door kept the prison.

Acts 12:5-6

*W*ho was this Herod and why was he persecuting the children of God? For you to understand what was really going on in this scripture and why the church today still needs to stand against Herod, allow me to give you a bit of background.

15 That which hath been is now; and that which is to be hath already been; and God requireth that which is past.

Ecclesiastes 3:15

That which is happening now already has been. What I want to bring to your attention is that what we are dealing with now in the twenty-first century, the church of early days has already dealt with. We are dealing with the same devil of the ancient world. The same devil that used Herod to persecute and vex the church back then is the same devil persecuting and vexing the church today.

The Herod spirit targets deliverers – those who would lead others out of captivity. During the days of Moses that spirit rose up through Pharaoh and influenced him to murder the male children born to the Israelites. By the grace of the Almighty, the deliverer, Moses, slipped through his hands. The Herod spirit is a brutal and bloodthirsty spirit that has no qualms with murdering babies and small children.

I realized that whenever the name Herod is mentioned in the Bible it always spells trouble for the children of God. Herod is a name used by several kings of the Herodian Dynasty of the Roman province of Judea. The founder of

> *The Herod spirit targets deliverers – those who would lead others out of captivity.*

the dynasty was Herod the Great. His father Antipater was Julius Caesar's procurator over Judea, Samaria and Galilee.

He was an Idumaean - a descendant of Esau. The Idumaeans came up out of the Negeb in southern Palestine about 125 BC and became

Jewish by religion although the Jews considered them as only half Jews

Herod the Great was appointed procurator (or, governor) in Galilee at the age of twenty-five. He was given a tetrarchy which was a quarter of a Roman province. Mark Antony made him King of Palestine and Augustus Caesar enlarged his territory. Herod did not become King until he captured Jerusalem in 37 BC.

He had a passion for architecture and built up the capital city of Jerusalem greatly. He was given permission to take Zerubbabel's temple down to its foundation and built up the temple to gain favor and access to the public genealogies so that he could destroy the genealogy of the expected Messiah. He financed the building of the temple himself.

He had nine wives and killed his wife Marianne as well as his own son. This Herod appears in Matthew 2:1-23. The Bible says that he was around seventy years of age when Jesus was born yet he was threatened by this baby's birth. He knew and his advisors confirmed, that a messiah or king was to be born although he didn't know when it would come to pass. When this boy was born he was told that the king had been born. He called for his advisors and all the spiritual leaders of that time to investigate the matter because he knew that the scriptures foretold his coming in the same way we know that Jesus is coming back again. The king's arrival threatened a king who was seventy years of age. Herod the Great tried to kill this young king and the Bible shows us that God was able to contain that threat. Herod was not able to discover where the child had been born. In his anger he sent his people out to kill every male child two years old and under. Again the deliverer, Jesus, slipped through this spirit's hands. While trying to kill Jesus, Herod the Great was attacked by sickness and died. Joseph and his family were exiles in Egypt until Herod's death.

The second Herod - Herod Archelaus - was the eldest of Herod's three sons who succeeded him. His mother was a Samaritan woman named Malthace. Herod wanted Archelaus on the throne after his death but fifty Jewish leaders sailed to Rome to protest against this. The emperor Augustus refused to allow him to reign as king but made him governor of half the kingdom: Samaria, Judea and Idumaea. His brothers were given the rest of the territories. Archelaus overstretched his authority which resulted in revolts. He tried to stop the revolts with cruel acts and terrorism. One Passover he slew three thousand protesting Jews and filled the temple with dead bodies. He was cruel and tyrannical, sensual in the extreme, a hypocrite and a plotter.

The Roman emperor Augustus eventually ended his reign and banished him to Vienne in Gaul (France) in response to complaints from the Jewish and Samaritan aristocracy.

Matthew 2:22 says that, after the death of Herod the Great, Joseph decided not to settle in Bethlehem but instead went into Galilee with his young family to avoid Archelaus.

The third Herod we encounter in the Bible is Herod Antipas who was the son of Herod the Great and his wife Malthace; he was a full brother of Archelaus and a half brother of Philip. He was made tetrarch of Galilee and Perea by his father and Emperor Augustus of Rome.

History calls him a wily sneak and Jesus called him a "fox" in Luke 13:32. He committed sly, selfish crimes that lacked principle. While visiting his half brother Philip, he eloped with Philip's wife, Herodias. He was first married to Phasaelis, a daughter of Aretas IV, an Arabian leader whom he divorced in order to marry Herodias. John the Baptist preached against this scandal in Mark 6:18 and lost his head as a result.

Antipas was perplexed by Jesus because it was rumoured that Jesus was John the Baptist come to life (Luke 9:7; Matthew 14:2). Antipas was in Jerusalem and had come from his territory of Galilee during Jesus' final week. He had Jesus appear before him for one of the trials before the crucifixion (Luke 23:5-12). The Gospel of Luke states that Jesus was first brought before Pontius Pilate for trial, since Pilate was the governor of Roman Judea, which encompassed Jerusalem where Jesus was arrested. Pilate initially handed him over to Antipas, in whose territory Jesus had been most active, but Antipas sent him back to Pilate's court.

In 39 AD Antipas was accused by his nephew Herod Agrippa I of conspiracy against the new Roman emperor Caligula, who sent him into exile in Gaul with Herodias.

Agrippa was the grandson of Herod the Great and son of Aristobulus IV who was killed by his father Herod the Great. Agrippa was educated in Rome as were all Herodian Princes and very zealous of Jewish law.

He was the last ruler with the royal title reigning over Judea and the father of Herod Agrippa II - the last king from the Herodian dynasty. Agrippa became one of the most powerful kings of the east. His domain more or less equaled that which was held by his grandfather Herod the Great. In the Bible, he is the king named Herod in Acts 12:1. Christian and Jewish historians take different views of this king, with the Christians largely opposing Agrippa and the Jews largely favoring him.

Acts 12 relates that he was eaten by worms, after God struck him for accepting the praise of flatterers who compared him to a god. Luke claimed that the gruesome death was retribution for Agrippa's blasphemous acceptance of the flattery of a delegation from Tyre and Sidon who said his voice was "the voice of a god, not of a man." (Acts. 12.20–24)

Agrippa II, son of Herod Agrippa, was asked, with his sister Berenice, by the Roman Procurator of Judea, Porcius Festus, to assist in the mini-trial of Apostle Paul.

With this background in place we can better understand the events of Acts 12.

¹Now about that time Herod the king stretched out his hand to harass some from the church. ²Then he killed James the brother of John with the sword. ³And because he saw that it pleased the Jews, he proceeded further to seize Peter also. Now it was during the Days of Unleavened Bread. ⁴So when he had arrested him, he put him in prison, and delivered him to four squads of soldiers to keep him, intending to bring him before the people after Passover. ⁵Peter was therefore kept in prison, but constant[a] prayer was offered to God for him by the church. ⁶And when Herod was about to bring him out, that night Peter was sleeping, bound with two chains between two soldiers; and the guards before the door were keeping the prison. ⁷Now behold, an angel of the Lord stood by him, and a light shone in the prison; and he struck Peter on the side and raised him up, saying, "Arise quickly!" And his chains fell off his hands. ⁸Then the angel said to him, "Gird yourself and tie on your sandals"; and so he did. And he said to him, "Put on your garment and follow me." ⁹So he went out and followed him, and did not know that what was done by the angel was real, but thought he was seeing a vision. [10] When they were past the first and the second guard posts, they came to the iron gate that leads to the city, which opened to them of its own accord; and they went out and went down one street, and immediately the angel departed from him. [11] And when Peter had come to himself, he said, "Now I know for certain that the Lord has sent His angel, and has delivered me from the hand of Herod and from all the expectation of the Jewish people.

Acts 12:1-11

In his pursuit of popularity Herod Agrippa killed James, the son of Zebedee. When the Jews applauded he went after Peter. In the midst of this persecution the church of Corinth found the key to deal with Herod.

With Peter on death row, the people of God gathered together. I call that fateful night "Peter's night." They knew that the battle was not against flesh and blood. They knew he was going to kill Peter brutally. They had witnessed how he had killed James. It was common knowledge that Herod was brutal and dangerous, but God revealed the prescript-tion to deal with the spirit behind this man in a wonderful way. The prescription was fervent prayer.

We cannot play games because there is a Herod in our times.

That which is has been. We cannot play games because there is a Herod in our times. This Herod might not be the same person but the spirit is the same. The prayers of the people who gathered together that fateful night inspired my life. For as long as I am living I know there is a spirit of Herod somehow, someway. That is why the children of God have dead financial lives. They have dead marriages and dead careers. Herod is still vexing the church even today.

There is a prescription to deal with Herod. It's not AK47s, looking good in new suites or driving fancy cars. It is not giving oil and water. It's nothing like that. It is earnest prayer. I want to give you the tablet that can stop Herod from vexing your family and your society. It is called fervent prayer.

I heard Jesus say, "Pray so that you may not fall into temptation." He said this because Herod sends his stuff to stop us from reaching our destiny. When we come together as a church in one accord, even though we might not see it with our naked eyes, I know someway, somehow, somebody's family is being delivered from Herod. This Herod is a liar and God has given us the grace to deal with the Herod of South Africa and the Herods of all the nations at large. Ladies and gentlemen, the church cannot win the battle without prayer.

There is a prescription to deal with Herod. It is called fervent prayer.

29

Never look good and fail to pray or the devil will play with your stuff. Never drive good and fail to pray because your car will lack petrol. Never work good and not pray because you will earn but not afford. Let us gather together as saints to pray and confuse the power of Herod. In our times we are vexed and frustrated and we come to church singing losing songs. We come to church looking like failures because Herod is still vexing the church. You come to church serving a mighty God yet you are achieving nothing because Herod is large and in charge. How about we come together like the church of Corinth?

The church has always come together without an agenda and yet Herod always has an agenda for the church. He knows who to kill and he knows who to abort. He doesn't bother himself with small fish. He goes for Moses and Jesus, for James and for the Peters because he knows that once you deal with these ones, you have dealt with the church at large. When you see pastors struggling financially, the attack is not for them - it's for the flock. When you see pastors divorcing, the enemy is after the flock.

31 *Then Jesus said unto them, "All ye shall be offended because of Me this night; for it is written: 'I will smite the Shepherd, and the sheep of the flock shall be scattered abroad.'*
Matthew 26:31

Herod knows that if he smites the shepherd the flock will scatter. I refuse in my time to see another pastor failing. I refuse in my time to see another pastor broke. These are the people that are supposed to dominate the space. Let us come together and pray. We have all faced trouble. We are all the same. Don't talk about me - pray with me. Don't gossip about me - pray for me. Don't judge me - pray with me. The devil I'm fighting is the same devil you're fighting.

Church, it is time to unite and know who we are fighting. Don't fight me because I am not your enemy. I am not the one who made you poor. It is Herod who is vexing the church. It is not your mother-in-law who hates you or your neighbour who is trying to bewitch you - it is Herod.

20 For where two or three are gathered together in my name, there am I in the midst of them.

Matthew 18:20

14 If my people, which are called by my name, shall humble themselves, and pray, and seek my face, and turn from their wicked ways; then will I hear from heaven, and will forgive their sin, and will heal their land.

2 Chronicles 7:14

The Lord wants to heal our nations. He just needs us to pray. My assignment is to expose this spirit of Herod that has been hidden from us for so long and to teach believers the art of prayer. We have pointed fingers and blamed one another for too long. It's time to expose the real culprit. It is Herod who is vexing the church and killing our marriages. He has been destroying our finances and killing our churches. He is killing our brothers. There are so many anointed people running without finishing their race and dying without honour. It is time for Herod to be destroyed. He has pleased his master and it's now time for the church to please God with their prayers. Politics has failed us. Smart and beautiful people have failed us but prayer will never fail us.

Peter's night is that night when the church is in charge. It's a night where prison doors are opened and innocent people are released from incarceration. Peter's night is a night when angels are released to help the children of God because of their prayers. It's a night when the righteous wake up with a testimony not realizing what has happened. They think they are dreaming when they wake up with a lot of money in their pockets.

When we pray no spiritual wives or husbands can visit the men and women of God because these foul spirits are scattered and displaced. Prayer leaves them roaming around aimlessly and confounded.

A beautiful thing about prayer is that there is no distance to it. You can pray in Johannesburg and get results in Giyani. Never be too lazy to pray for you do not know what you are doing when you set your mind to pray. The church is too busy to pray. It takes humble people to pray. When we advertise miracles and healing the church overflows with people but this season doesn't call for such people. It needs people who know who Herod is and who are willing to come together for prayer.

The Lord is my shepherd. I shall not want. Let all that is within me bless the Lord! In this season I will sing a joyful song because I know that when the day comes I will be singing, *"This is the day that the Lord has made!"* I'm going to rejoice because the joy of the Lord is my strength. I don't have to see the manifestation to dance. As long as I pray, I know I will see it. I know that when I pray He hears and when He hears He answers. He's got ears, He's got eyes and He's got a mouth. He can speak and He is speaking to you right now. He can see what is happening. He has heard of our afflictions.

God has so much in store for you child of God but it depends on how you align yourself. If you are with God those things you seek will come to you but if you chase after them, they will run from you. It's time to change direction. Chase after God and things will start to chase after you.

Herod needs to know that we have uncovered his scheme. We are that church that has an agenda. We have learnt a few things from him. When he gathers with his people, he is targeting James. After he's done with James he goes for Peter. As the church we must recognize the schemes of Herod and begin to stand against

> *I don't have to see the manifestation to dance for, as long as I pray, I know I will see it*

them. We have to refuse poverty. We do not have to sell water for us to be well. We must sell the product Jesus for us to be happy. I sell more than oil. I sell King Jesus Christ and you can buy Him without money. I know that when you have him your life will never be the same. He has no expiry date. He is forever a king and will look after you even when you are sleeping, driving or in the shower. In the valley of the shadow of death he will not leave you or forsake you.

¹ "Ho! Everyone who thirsts, come to the waters; and you who have no money, come, buy and eat. Yes, come, buy wine and milk without money and without price. ² Why do you spend money for what is not bread, and your wages for what does not satisfy? Listen carefully to Me, and eat what is good, and let your soul delight itself in abundance.
Isaiah 55:1-2 (NKJV)

Let us touch and agree on a few things. Herod is a liar. You cannot go five years without a job. If Herod can give jobs to his people, our God can give us jobs. We've got to silence this Herod in the name of Jesus. My agenda is to see you prosper. It is to see you established in your business or becoming a boss where you are working. My agenda is to see you marrying well and happy in everything you do. The reason you were not happy was because the devil was vexing the church. You just might be the Peter or James of your congergation.

We want to see churches flourishing. How can churches exist for twenty years and fail to own a piece of land. A poor church has no voice. It's time we agree. If silver and gold belong to our Father, we must own land. We must not owe the bank. Why is it that Christians are owing everybody? The devil is a liar!

8 Owe no man any thing, but to love one another: for he that loveth another hath fulfilled the law.

Romans 13:8

We are the kings and rulers on this earth – a royal priesthood. Herod is in trouble when we get together to enforce our kingdom rights. There is nothing impossible for you as a child of the Most High God. You shall eat the best of the land and it shall be well with you and your house.

If you've been crying for too long and are ready to silence Herod I invite you to embark on this journey with me as I teach you the art of prayer.

What Is Prayer?

Chapter One

Prayer is a beautiful thing. Every time you do it the right way, there's an inner joy that fulfills you. In Luke 22:43 an angel from heaven appeared to Jesus and strengthened him. That was after Jesus prayed a prayer that was in line with the will of God. Prayer is supposed to be offered up in a secret place for God to answer it in public. That could mean that it begins in the heart. It is not supposed to be a show or a religious mask worn to impress others. Prayer is intimacy with the Lord himself. The spiritual engagement that takes place in the secret place will eventually be witnessed as tangible results by almost everyone around you.

Prayer can be composed of the same words again and again

In prayer man and God are in a meeting that must be concluded with consensus. After the last supper in the twenty-sixth chapter of Matthew, Jesus took his disciples to a place called Gethsemane. He instructed them to wait there while he, Peter and the two sons of Zebedee went further for a prayer session. He was in great sorrow and we are told that he left the three men three times and that each time he prayed the same words again and again.

⁴⁴ And he left them, and went away again, and prayed the third time, saying the same words.

Matthew 26:44

This proves to us that prayer can be composed of the same words again and again. It is not about impressing God with a lot of empty words and jargon, but it is about expressing your innermost thoughts before the Lord.

Prayer is about talking to God concerning a situation. Scripture always proves that when you pray God must be involved. Everywhere in the bible, no matter how challenging the situation, everything called a prayer is directed to the Lord. In *Matthew 6:9-13* Jesus taught them how to pray. We are to approach "our Father". If we are approaching our Father it suggests that He is the one who must attend to the matter.

Never waste your time praying against demons or negotiating with them. You must, instead, use your authority and power as a believer to deal with demons. You have to say Amen to this! It is amazing that there is no record of Jesus praying when he had to deal with demons. He just commanded them without any struggle and all kinds of spirits would have to obey him. When it came to speaking to God he prayed and sometimes fasted for more empowerment from the Lord. From today I see your prayer life changing. You can no longer waste your time negotiating with demons in your life but you must start commanding. Authority has been given to you by Christ's command. Exercise your faith and see how powerful you are. It blessed my life to know that I carry power within me as a child of God.

Never undermine the power of prayer because it has the potential to shift atmospheres. Prophet Elijah shifted the atmosphere by prayer. From a clear blue sky in a drought-ridden land a small cloud appeared, then several large clouds that brought heavy rain. *Elijah said to Ahab. "As surely as the LORD lives, no rain or dew will fall few years unless I command it."*

17 Elias was a man subject to like passions as we are, and he prayed earnestly that it might not rain: and it rained not on the earth by the space of three years and six months. 18 And he prayed again, and the heaven gave rain, and the earth brought forth her fruit.

James 5:17-18

When you pray the right way you become a candidate for answered prayer. Upgrade your prayer level.

What is Prayer?

Prayer is a way for men to communicate with God. It was designed by God to enable humanity to make our requests known unto the Lord. It is a spiritual sacrifice and fruit of our lips. When man makes an effort to reach God - God responds to man. Prayer is communion between God and man. It is a sincere, sensible, affectionate pouring out of the soul to God, through Christ

6 Be careful for nothing; but in every thing by prayer and supplication with thanksgiving let your requests be made known unto God.
Philippians 4:6

It is very clear that by prayer and supplication we make our requests known before our God. Time in prayer is not wasted. Make the time and pour your heart unto the Lord for He cares for you.

It is not prayer unless it involves God and the man. It is not prayer until there are answers. Man has to communicate his/her heart and God has to answer or communicate His will back to man. That is what we call prayer.

Prayer without worship is a complaint

God + man + communication = prayer

Prayer without worship is a complaint

40

The Significance of Prayer

A prayerful person will never lack answers from the Lord. The significance of prayer is that it can change any situation when it is done in faith. Prayer without faith is just a loud sound without communicating your desire unto the Lord. There is no answer for such a prayer. Never make the mistake of associating a loud voice from a person that is supposed to be praying with a heartfelt prayer that involves talking to God. If it is prayer it must involve you, God, worship, faith and your request, which results in your answer.

My wife Alicia Ngoveni likes to say that money and education cannot deal with every situation we come across in life. There are spiritual forces and principalities that can only be broken and dealt with by exercising spiritual authority. You get your authority activated in prayer.

11 Put on the whole armour of God, that ye may be able to stand against the wiles of the devil. 12 For we wrestle not against flesh and blood, but against principalities, against powers, against the rulers of the darkness of this world, against spiritual wickedness in high places.

Ephesians 6:11-12

Why Do We Pray?

There are many different reasons for prayer.

- We pray so we may be able to stand against the schemes of the devil (Ephesians 6:11).
- We pray so we may not fall into temptation (Matthew 26:41).
- We pray so we may gain victory.
- We pray so we may hear God (1 John 14,15).
- We pray so we may be strengthened by the Spirit of the Lord (Luke 22:46)
- We pray so we may praise and worship the Lord.
- We pray so we may call things that are not there as though they are there (Romans 4:17).
- We pray so God may grant the desires of our hearts (Psalm 37:4).

It is imperative that a child of God acknowledge the life of prayer and commit to such. Where there's prayer there's peace. When you know that God is in charge your life becomes stress free. Wait a minute. Jesus said, "Let your will be done" meaning that God's will must prevail. When you pray you pour out your desire but you must allow the will of God to overcome your desire. Prayer, therefore, aligns us to the will of God and liberates us from being stuck in the desires of our flesh.

> *When you pray you pour out your desire but you must allow the will of God to overcome your desire*

Jesus Taught Us How to Pray

Chapter Two

*P*rayer is not supposed to be done randomly; it has a form and is an art. Every machine has its own manual that is designed to help the users to employ the machine effectively. When the instructions in the manual are not heeded the machine might still work but not effectively. You can be effective in your prayer life by following the guidelines. The disciples observed Jesus praying and probably noticed a big difference between his prayers and their own. They asked him to teach them how to pray.

1 And it came to pass, that, as he was praying in a certain place, when he ceased, one of his disciples said unto him, Lord, teach us to pray, as John also taught his disciples. 2 And he said unto them, When ye pray, say, Our Father which art in heaven, Hallowed be thy name. Thy kingdom come. Thy will be done, as in heaven, so in earth. 3 Give us day by day our daily bread. 4 And forgive us our sins; for we also forgive every one that is indebted to us. And lead us not into temptation; but deliver us from evil.

Luke 11:1-4

Our Father in Heaven

This has to do with your relationship with the Lord. You are not going to be apologetic when you speak to your father. Have a winning attitude. Tell God that He is your father. You are going to direct your prayer to the father. I love this. Hallelujah! We have access to the father who is ready to listen to us at all times. The songwriter says, "What a privilege and an honour to worship at your throne, to be called into your presence as your own...."

15 For ye have not received the spirit of bondage again to fear; but ye have received the Spirit of adoption, whereby we cry, Abba, Father.

Romans 8:15

You and I are the sons of God. Prayer is talking to God therefore it must begin with God.

Hallowed Be Your Name

This has to do with worshiping the Lord. It is to render sacred, to consecrate. The proper meaning of this word "hallow" is to make holy - to reverence God as a holy God. One of our major roles as God`s children is to worship Him. We are the chosen generation - a royal priesthood. Before you present your request before Him, first acknowledge His holiness.

⁶ Honour and majesty are before him: strength and beauty are in his sanctuary.

Psalm 96:6

Be an altar of worship for His presence to dwell in you. Bear in mind that you can only attract what you worship. Worship first then He will listen to you.

> *Be an altar of worship for his presence to dwell in*

I was told of a man who wanted to meet one of the legendary soccer icons in South Africa. The man tried by all means to make an appointment without success. One day there was a soccer match where the legend was supposed to be one of the VIPs of the day. This man bought a VIP ticket so he could sit next to the legend and hence get a chance to have a chat with him. The man's wishes turned into a nightmare. Something came up as the legend was making his way to the soccer match and he had to attend to some family issues instead. To cut my story short one day they again happened to be in the same place. The man forced his way into the room where the soccer legend was. He asked for the opportunity to talk to the legend on the basis that he so admired him and had aspired to be like him from his youth. With an odd look the legend offered him two minutes of his time as he was too busy.

45

The man began to tell the legend how he was so inspired by him. He told him about how much he had wanted to be like him when he was young because of the extraordinary soccer skills that he displayed. He even told him the name they used to call him during that time. This was basically worship to the legend. Now, the legend, from being nonchalant, began to smile. He quickly arranged for a photo shoot with the man. He gave him a parcel which included a beautiful soccer t-shirt written the legend`s name. Remember that the man was given two minutes. Now the legend didn't want to let go of the

Worship will have God give you more than you reques-ted

man. He asked for his name and contact number. It was as if they were now friends. Worship will have God give you more than you requested. Just go ahead and do like the man. Worship the Lord your God!

Your Kingdom Come

You cannot separate God from His kingdom. He is kingdom oriented and consumed in the kingdom agenda.

> **6 For unto us a child is born, unto us a son is given: and the government shall be upon his shoulder: and his name shall be called Wonderful, Counsellor, The mighty God, The everlasting Father, The Prince of Peace.**
> **Isaiah 9:6**

God wants us to be restored to our original state as humanity. After man fell from grace he lost his kingdom orientation and the kingdom of darkness was now reigning in him.

The power of governing the kingdom is vested in our God as the king of the kingdom. Every kingdom has a king. Jesus is our king because the government of the kingdom was placed upon his shoulder (Isaiah 9:6). Government signifies the body with the power to make or enforce laws to control a country or kingdom. If God can control your environment it is easy for Him to give you what you want. Acknowledge His kingdom in your prayer so that it may rule your space. If there was something else dominating your space before, it will have to bow to the greater kingdom. It feels good to have the kingdom of God reigning in your life as there is no failure in this kingdom. Nothing is impossible when you abide under its laws. It is a kingdom of abundance. Everything you need is in it.

Remember how Jesus began his ministry. He went around by the seashore proclaiming, *"Repent for the kingdom of God is at hand!"* This signifies that in your prayers you should invite God to take over. Praying *"Your kingdom come o Lord"* means you want the kingdom and its supreme ruler - the king – to dominate in your world. Every knee must bow and every tongue must confess that Jesus is the Lord.

Your Will Be Done

Like I mentioned earlier, the will of God must always defeat our own. God's will always comes with promotion because it is of a higher standard than ours. It completes us internally and sets us up for the glory of God. Praying *"Your will be done o Lord"* signifies selfless acknowledgement of God as supreme.

Give Us Our Daily Bread

When God is present you can put your requests on the table. Bread signifies provision. We are petitioning God for our physical needs relating to our finances, health, etc.

O—ᴡ
God's will always comes with promotion because it is of a higher standard than ours

7 Ask, and it shall be given you; seek, and ye shall find; knock, and it shall be opened unto you:
Matthew 7:7

God has nothing against us asking from Him. It is His will that we ask because He is able to do far abundantly more than we could ever ask or imagine. Never assume that it will be done for you if you never placed an order. I have realised that it takes pride for a man not to ask. It takes a humble man to pray and ask from the Lord. Asking is in the Word. We are doing the will of God when we do it. Never feel less after asking from the Lord because Jesus said, *"Ask and it will be given to you."* It can be considered wrong and presumptuous to ask for things that you were not promised. Christians have been known as people who ask a lot but this is a result of the abundant promises God has for us.

He said, "Ask anything in my name and it shall be given to you." It only becomes a problem when you walk around asking from people. They will undermine you beca-

It takes a humble man to pray and ask from the Lord

use they don't have what it takes to answer your prayers. Only God can do that. David said I have not seen a righteous man being forsaken by God or his children begging for food. Every time you see people praying and asking from the Lord, know that He said, "Ask and it will be given." They are not asking from you so don`t stress. They won't take everything from the storeroom of the Lord either. Don`t stop them but rather join them and plead your own case.

The Lord gives us our daily bread. I just love it when God begins to answer prayers. He is both faithful and able to do so. It is His will to give you what you need. Never let anything deceive you. God wants you blessed, He wants you happy, and He wants to see you successful. The devil is a liar. You shall have what you are asking God for. Say Amen to this.

His promises are yes and amen. It blesses me that Jesus would say, "*Ask, and you will receive, that your joy may be full.*" (John 16:24b NKJV).

Pastors have condemned the attitude of asking from the Lord. We ask so that our joy may be fulfilled. The Lord gives us our daily bread. This thing is a daily matter Baby so no one should stop it. I encourage you to find your corner and tell Him what you want. He is your father. He expects you to do so. Love Him as you do so.

Forgive Us Our Sins As We Forgive Others

It is amazing how we would love for God to forgive us when in our hearts we have so much against other people. The greatest deliverance in your life comes when you are able to let go of the past. You will be free from hurt, competition, jealousy, witchcraft, and curses. Unforgiveness is caused by refusing to let go of past events in your life. I have discovered that most people that are enemies in life are people who once extremely loved one another. People you are struggling to forgive are usually the people you need the most for your life to go to the next level.

25 And when ye stand praying, forgive, if ye have ought against any: that your Father also which is in heaven may forgive you your trespasses.

Mark 11:25

Moreover, this ministry of forgiveness is what Jesus is all about. He died in order to forgive us our sins. There is better life in God - a life with peace in your heart. You have so much precious stuff to keep in your heart rather than filling it with memories of people and things that hurt you.

23 Guard your heart above all else, for it determines the course of your life.

Proverbs 4:23

Choose to live a life of joy, peace and happiness. Forgiving others is also to acknowledge that no one is perfect in life. A familiar saying that I grew up hearing puts it this way, *"Do unto others what you would like them to do unto you"*. I normally say before you deal with others concerning the wrong they have done to you, kindly consider if you've ever wronged anyone before. If you were afforded a chance to wrong others and be forgiven, you too must be

Before you deal with others concerning the wrong they have done to you, kindly consider if you've ever wronged anyone before. If you were afforded a chance to wrong others then be able to forgive

able to forgive. Forgiving others glorifies the Lord and will pave a way for you to receive your answer. As you pray, don't allow your answer to be withheld because you have failed to forgive. Let go and let God fill you with laughter. Say Amen to this.

Lead Us Not Into Temptation

This is one of the most neglected portions of prayer. Temptation is the most dangerous tool of the enemy. He used it against Adam and Eve and was successful. He managed to take them down. He also tried to take down King Jesus with the same tactic but it didn't work. You need to understand this. Jesus had to deal with the power of temptation and win because failure would have aborted his mission. God Himself doesn't tempt but He can test us so He can promote us.

God Himself doesn't tempt but He can test us so He can promote us

4 Then was Jesus led up of the Spirit into the wilderness to be tempted of the devil.

Matthew 4:1

23 The steps of a good man are ordered by the Lord: and he delighteth in his way..

Psalm 37:23

As you pray ask that the Lord must not lead you to temptation but, instead, guide your footsteps to green pastures and lead you beside still waters. May your life progress and may you live to kiss your destiny. Say Amen to this.

The Difference Between a Test And Temptation

Tests and temptation are not the same thing and it is very important for a believer to understand the difference between the two. Tests are for elevation yet temptation is meant to take you down

Test	Temptation
➤ It is the work of the Lord	➤ It is the work of the devil
➤ It is meant to approve you for new level	➤ It is meant to reduce your standard
➤ It is done with love	➤ There is no implications of love
➤ Promotion after	➤ Downfall after
➤ Glorified after	➤ Dishonour after
➤ It can only edify you	➤ This takes your rights

You Ask Amiss

Chapter Three

2 Ye lust, and have not: ye kill, and desire to have, and cannot obtain: ye fight and war, yet ye have not, because ye ask not. 3 Ye ask, and receive not, because ye ask amiss, that ye may consume it upon your lusts.

James 4:2-3

F rom this scripture we get a clear-cut answer for why some prayers are not answered.

Don't be too big to ask from the Lord. If you haven't asked, it's impossible for God to give you anything. Like I said earlier, God is not bothered by your prayer requests. You can never deplete His limitless supply by asking for too much. It is important to follow the leading of the Holy Spirit in every area of your life because God cannot empower what He never started. He will not answer prayers that are contrary to His will.

> *Don't be too big to ask from the Lord*

The challenge is that we are more consumed by our own desires than by the will of God. The purpose of God is always considered last therefore it reduces the chances of God answering our prayers. Praying amiss implies that you are not considering the will of God but only focusing on what you want to receive from Him. Your goal is mainly your own pleasure. You will always be responsible for your own projects but God will always finish what He has begun. He finds pleasure in answering prayers that are in line with His will. If you stay away from lust, envies, murder, and other forms of sin, and align your motives with the will of God, you will not miss your answer. I declare that you are not going to pray amiss. Just keep praying. I see the Lord answering you faster than you expected.

When Are We Supposed to Pray?

17 Pray without ceasing,
1 Thessalonians 5:17

A lot of the time people pray when they are under pressure. I have seen people happily living prayerless lives when things are going well with them. The moment things turn bitter they begin to incline themselves towards a life of prayer. You are not supposed to be pushed to prayer by circumstances or fear.

When Paul encouraged the Thesssalonians to "*pray without ceasing*" he did not necessarily mean that they were to pray non-stop. He meant that they should always have a desire to do it. I encourage you to make time for fellowship with the Lord. The life of prayer will always serve you with divine revelation - the secrets of Heaven. It will give you access to the mysteries of God. In Matthew 17:2 when Peter, James and John were with Jesus on the mountain they saw Jesus being transfigured. They also saw Elijah and Moses appear before Jesus. There is a lot of amazing stuff that is not seen by just anyone. It can only be accessed through fellowship with Him in prayer. I encourage you to live a life of prayer. It is of great benefit to you.

The Early Church's Victory

When we read the inspired history of the church as recorded by Luke (under the inspiration of the Holy Spirit) in the Acts of the Apostles, what do we find? We find a story of constant victory - a story of perpetual progress.

47 Praising God, and having favour with all the people. And the Lord added to the church daily such as should be saved.

The Lord added to the church daily

Acts 2:47

4 Howbeit many of them which heard the word believed; and the number of the men was about five thousand.

Acts 4:4

NE Ngoveni

**¹⁴ *And believers were the more added to the
Lord, multitudes both of men and women.***

Acts 5:14

In addition Luke, in Acts 6:7 states, "*And the
word of God increased: and the number of the
disciples multiplied in Jerusalem greatly; and a
great company of the priests were obedient to the
faith.*"

As we read through all the twenty-eight chapters of the book of Acts, we find the same note of
victory. I once went through the Acts of the
Apostles marking every verse that spoke of victory
in every chapter. Without one exception, the
triumphant shout of victory rang out in every single
chapter. How different the history of the church as
here recorded is from the history of the church of
Jesus Christ in our modern times. Take, for example,
that first statement, 'The Lord added to the church
daily (that's every day) such as should be saved."
Nowadays, if we have a revival once a year with
an accession of fifty or sixty members to our
numbers and spend the rest of the year slipping
back to where we were before, we think we are
doing pretty well. In those days there was a revival
all the time and accessions every day of those who
not only "hit the trail" but "were really being saved."

What could be the reason for this difference
between the early church and the church of Jesus
Christ today? Someone will answer, "It's because
there is so much opposition today." Ah, but there
was opposition in those days too – more bitter,

58

more determined, more relentless opposition. In fact, in comparison, that which you and I meet today is but child's play. The early church went right on beating down all opposition, surmounting every obstacle and conquering every foe. They were always victorious from Jerusalem to Rome in the face of such firmly entrenched and extreme heathenism and unbelief. I repeat the question, "Why is there such a big difference between us and them?" If you will turn to the chapters from which I have already quoted, you will get your answer.

Steadfast Prayer

⁴² And they continued steadfastly in the apostles' doctrine and fellowship, and in breaking of bread, and in prayers.

Acts 2:42

That is a picture - very brief but very descriptive - of the early church. It was a praying church. It was a church that prayed, not merely occasionally, but they all "continued steadfastly...in prayers." They all prayed, not a select few, but the whole membership of the church. They all prayed continuously with steadfast determination.

Acts 6:4 gives us the rest of the answer.

⁴ But we will give ourselves continually to prayer....

Acts 6:4

That is a picture of the apostolic ministry. It was a praying ministry - a ministry that "gave themselves continually to prayer." If we translate that Greek word as it is translated in the former passage (Acts 2:42) we get, "They continued steadfastly in prayer." A praying church and a praying ministry. Such a church and such a ministry can achieve anything that needs to be achieved. It will go steadily on, beating down all opposition, surmounting every obstacle, and conquering every foe, just as the church did in the days of the apostles.

Present-Day Departure From Prayer

There is nothing else in which the church and the ministry of today or, to be more explicit, you and I, have departed more notably and more lamentably from the apostolic precedent than in this matter of prayer. We do not live in a praying age. A very considerable proportion of the membership of our evangelical churches today do not believe even theoretically in prayer. Many of them now believe in prayer as having a beneficial "reflex influence," that is, as benefitting the person who prays - a sort of lifting yourself up by your spiritual bootstraps. As for prayer bringing anything to pass that would not have come to pass without it, they do not believe this. Many of them frankly say so. Even some of our "modern ministers" say so. I believe the vast majority in our evangelical churches are not making use of this mighty instrument that God has put into our hands. As I said, we do not live in a praying age. We live in an age of hustle and bustle; of man's efforts and man's determination; of man's confidence in himself and in his own power to achieve things; an age of human organization and human machinery; human push and human scheming; and human achievement. In the things of God human achievement means no real achievement at all.

I think it would be perfectly safe to say that the church of Christ has never in all its history been so fully, so skillfully, so thoroughly, and so perfectly organised as it is today. Our machinery is wonderful. It is just perfect but, alas, it is machinery without power. When things don't go right, instead of going to the real source of our failure which is our neglect of dependence on God and His power, we look around to see if there is not some new organisation we can get up or some new wheel we can add to our machinery. We have too many wheels already. What we need is not so much some new organization or some new wheel, but "the Spirit of the living creature in the wheels" that we already possess (Ezekiel 1:20).

I believe that the devil stands and looks at the church today and laughs in his sleeve as he sees how its members depend on their own scheming and powers of organisation and skillfully devised machinery. "Ha, ha," he laughs, "You may have your Boy Scouts, your costly church edifices, your multi-thousand-dollar church organs, your brilliant university-bred preachers, your high-priced choirs, your gifted sopranos, and altos, and tenors, and basses, your wonderful quartets, your immense men's Bible classes, yes, and your Bible conferences, and your Bible institutes, and your special evangelistic services. It does not in the least trouble me, if you will only leave out the power of the Lord God Almighty." This power is sought and obtained by earnest, persistent, believing prayer that will not take no for an answer.

When the devil sees a man or woman who really believes in prayer, who knows how to pray, and who really does pray, and, above all, when he sees a whole church on its face before God in prayer - he trembles! He knows that his day in that church or community is at an end.

> *When the devil sees a man or woman who really believes in prayer, who knows how to pray, and who really does pray, and, above all, when he sees a whole church on its face before God in prayer, "he trembles"*

Hannah's Prayer

Chapter Four

¹ Now there was a certain man of Ramatha-imzo-phim, of mount Ephraim, and his name was Elkanah, the son of Jeroham, the son of Elihu, the son of Tohu, the son of Zuph, an Ephrathite: ² And he had two wives; the name of the one was Hannah, and the name of the other Peninnah: and Peninnah had children, but Hannah had no children. ³ And this man went up out of his city yearly to worship and to sacrifice unto the Lord of hosts in Shiloh. And the two sons of Eli, Hophni and Phinehas, the priests of the Lord, were there. ⁴ And when the time was that Elkanah offered, he gave to Peninnah his wife, and to all her sons and her daughters, portions: ⁵ But unto Hannah he gave a worthy portion; for he loved Hannah: but the Lord had shut up her womb.

1 Samuel 1:1-5

*H*annah's prayer has got a huge lesson concerning a human being's capability versus God's capability. If God has closed no one can open, however, the way in which Hannah dealt with her barrenness was interesting. Instead of trying physicians she just prayed. Elkanah could give as much as he could. Trust me he did everything within his ability to get the matter solved. It is normal to give everything to someone you love the most. When you are in a position of being loved, either by people or God, you are standing in a position of receiving a double portion from them. Love is always expressed by giving more. Be like Elkanah. If you love, give a double portion.

After her husband had failed her, Hannah approached God and forgot about everything. No amount of effort can open what God has closed, but prayer can.

⁶ *And her rival used to provoke her grievously to irritate her, because the LORD had closed her womb".*

1 Samuel 1:6

I want to believe that the most painful thing for Hannah was not her rival Penninah`s laughter, but it was her barrenness. Have you ever been in a situation that demands your attention more than anything else that is happening around you?

Her pain was more on the inside than on the outside. She concentrated more on the closed womb than on Penninah laughing at her and Elkanah giving her all he could. Nothing mattered except what she wanted. When you have an internal issue, let it concern you more than what people are saying. At times people that claim to love you can fail you by giving you things or saying words that make no difference to your situation. God will always give that which fulfills us from the inside.

He utters words that are spirit and life (John 6:63), words loaded with power and peace. His are words that bring healing from within. What a privilege to serve under such a God. Just to call him Daddy is an awesome thing. Oh how I love this God!

7 And as he did so year by year, when she went up to the house of the Lord, so she provoked her; therefore she wept, and did not eat. 8 Then said Elkanah her husband to her, Hannah, why weepest thou? and why eatest thou not? and why is thy heart grieved? am not I better to thee than ten sons?

1 Samuel 1:7-8

It sounds like Elkanah accepted the situation because he asks her if his love and what he is giving her is not enough? He sounds OK. Someimes people feel good when they give to you and you are not able to give back to them because it gives them a sense of power

Never allow people to keep giving you things while you are failing to give back. It will cause them to undermine you.

over you. Hannah could not settle for such. She wanted to give back also. She didn't just want to be a receiver. Never allow people to keep giving you things while you are failing to give back. It will cause them to undermine you.

> **⁷ The rich ruleth over the poor, and the borrower is servant to the lender.**
>
> **Proverbs 22:7**

Sometimes you have to make it clear to people around you that it is not about what they can do for you, but about what you can do for them. I discovered that the richest and greatest people in life are not the people who receive the most, but are the people who give the most. They might give in the form of a service, idea, money, etc.

The right answer begins with the right question. Elkanah's question clearly reveals that he was not in pain and that he expected Hannah to feel the same. Sometimes when people expect you to answer questions that would contradict your expectation from the Lord, do not answer. Ignore such a trap because it will have you compromise your heart's desire.

Sometimes you have to make it clear to people around you that it is not about what they can do for you, but about what you can do for them

> **²⁹ Let no corrupt communication proceed out of your mouth, but that which is good to the use of edifying, that it may minister grace unto the hearers.**
>
> **Ephesians 4:29**

May our good Lord grant your heart's desire as you pray. Continue to utter what you are believing for and have faith in God.

> **⁹ So Hannah rose up after they had eaten in Shiloh, and after they had drunk. Now Eli the priest sat upon a seat by a post of the temple of the Lord. ¹⁰ And she was in bitterness of soul, and prayed unto the Lord, and wept sore.**
>
> **1 Samuel 1:9-10**

I see Hannah doing the right thing all the way. The situation was tense yet nothing was able to stop her pouring her heart to the Lord. She cried before the Lord. Remember this, crying before the Lord is better than crying before man. You do not lose dignity by crying before your God. Pride has a way of stopping you from crying for your breakthrough before the Lord. I do not see her crying before Elkanah, her rival, or before the priest. She cried before the Lord. This was not a matter for man. She had to take her tears directly to the Lord.

> **⁸ You keep track of all my sorrows. You have collected all my tears in your bottle. You have recorded each one in your book.**
>
> **Psalm 56:8 (NLT)**

We know that in the Old Testament people had to have the priest present their petition before the Lord. He would ask for forgiveness for the people with them not even present. This intercession for the people would take place in the Holy of Holies. In this passage of scripture we see Hannah testing grace by accessing God on her own. I want to believe she was in the place where Eli was and actually talking to God Himself while the prophet was observing her. I trust she bypassed the protocol. The priest was in the temple yet she could not say anything to him. She went straight to the Lord. She only acknowledged Eli when he asked her a question. When your case is too heavy, you must deal with God Himself for yourself. Grace came with those benefits. We can now access the Holy of Holies and approach His throne of grace with boldness by virtue of what Christ has done for us.

16 Let us therefore come boldly unto the throne of grace, that we may obtain mercy, and find grace to help in time of need.
Hebrews 4:16

If you are in a grave situation right now, I advise you to begin pouring out your heart before the Lord.

20 Now unto him that is able to do exceeding abundantly above all that we ask or think, according to the power that worketh in us,
Ephesians 3:20

We serve an awesome God.

11 And she vowed a vow, and said, O Lord of hosts, if thou wilt indeed look on the affliction

of thine handmaid, and remember me, and not forget thine handmaid, but wilt give unto thine handmaid a man child, then I will give him unto the Lord all the days of his life, and there shall no razor come upon his head.

1 Samuel 1:11

Hannah is amazing. She makes a deal - a promise to God. She promises to give all the glory back to Him. When you are desperate it is easy to make promises in order to gain favour. This Biblical account expounds something to us - that which the Lord gives must serve the purpose for which it was given. It must not be defiled.

Always be specific when you make your request known to God for He is not threatened by your requests. Hannah was clear. She wanted a son. As a person in need, you are in a position to mention what can satisfy you. Be humble enough to let God know of your expectation. Nothing is too big for the Lord God Almighty. He might have opened the womb but the gender of the child was determined by Hannah. Wherever you are, be able to open your mouth and say it precisely as you want it. Let God shine over what He has done in your life and have you sing songs about Him alone.

He might have opened the womb but the gender of the child was determined by Hannah

12 And it came to pass, as she continued praying before the Lord, that Eli marked her mouth. 13 Now Hannah, she spake in her heart; only her lips moved, but her voice was not heard: therefore Eli thought she had been drunken. 14 And Eli said unto her, How long wilt thou be drunken? put away thy wine from thee.

1 Samuel 1:12-14

Sometimes when you are in pain, you can be misunderstood by the very people that are supposed to help you get over that pain. Eli could not feel the pain she was going through, neither could he discern that she was not under the influence of wine or alcohol. He could not understand that Hannah was just in need and that he was the one to say a word for her situation to change. Her husband could not help much in this case but Eli could.

15 And Hannah answered and said, No, my lord, I am a woman of a sorrowful spirit: I have drunk neither wine nor strong drink, but have poured out my soul before the Lord. 16 Count not thine handmaid for a daughter of Belial: for out of the abundance of my complaint and grief have I spoken hitherto.

1 Samuel 1:15-16

You see, challenges can affect you to a point where they affect the way other people perceive you. Hannah was not drunk; she was just in pain. You have to be persistent with your desire. Don't beat around the bush but say what is in your heart. I need you to remember this whenever you pray. Never tell God more about your pain than what you want Him to do for you. He knows what you're going through and He expects you to ask Him for what you need. Coming to His presence and talking about how much pain you have serves no purpose. In His presence what matters most is not your pain but your victory. Hannah was so firm, "I want a son."

17 Then Eli answered and said, Go in peace: and the God of Israel grant thee thy petition that thou hast asked of him.
1 Samuel 1:17

Now this is clear. It will always be an easy job for a prophet or God to bless you after you have specified what you want. Eli was not able to release a blessing to Hannah until he understood that she was not drunk but pouring her heart to the Lord. She was then blessed with the desire of her heart.

Hannah's story is rich with several elements that lead to victory in prayer. I need you to take into consideration six things that allowed the Lord to honour Hannah's request.

1. Hannah Was Persistent

She was recorded year after year going to the feast with the same request before the Lord. Irrespective of what her rival was doing against her she continued to submit her request before Jehovah and cry for her success. I discovered that persistence does not happen automatically, but it is intentional. You choose to persist even when the circumstances do not allow. Sometimes you have to discipline yourself to be persistent.

> *Persistence does not happen automatically, but it is intentional. You choose to persist even when the circumstances do not allow.*

2. Hannah Trusted in The Lord

From the length of time that she waited to receive her answer from the Lord it is clear that she trusted the Lord. It was hard for her. This matter became the focal point of her prayers every time she was in God`s presence. It seems like Elkanah was also disturbed by her prayer strategy because he felt left out. You recall him asking Hannah "Am I not better than ten sons?" She chose to put her trust in the Lord and not in the ability of her husband.

3. Hannah Believed in God`s Prophet

Hannah prayed for years without receiving her breakthrough. She poured her heart out before the Lord. The amazing thing here is that although she prayed to God, it was not until the man of God Eli spoke a word over her situation, that she was able to access her breakthrough. I am persuaded that the key to your prosperity lies with your prophet. I want to believe that if Hannah had spoken to Eli as soon as she discovered that she was infertile, this matter would not have taken so long to be resolved. Eli`s word unlocked Hannah's womb. Your prophet is ordained by God for your prosperity.

20 And they rose early in the morning, and went forth into the wilderness of Tekoa: and as they went forth, Jehoshaphat stood and said, Hear me, O Judah, and ye inhabitants of Jerusalem; Believe in the LORD your God, so shall ye be established; believe his prophets, so shall ye prosper.

2 Chronicles 20:20

Believe in your prophet and you will prosper.

4. Hannah Was Specific

"If only God can give me a son," Hannah says. She could have said if only God can grant me a child. But she had what she wanted in mind. She never got weary of singing a song of what she believed God for. She wanted a son. Be able to compose a song out of what you are believing God for and sing it! Let your wishes be known more than your fears.

5. Hannah Was Appreciative

She promised the Lord that if He would bless her with a son, no razor would touch his head, nor would he be defiled with wine. Instead, the child would be given back to God for the services of the kingdom. The child was named Samuel meaning *"that which the Lord had given"*. The child was consecrated as Hannah had promised. It is important to fulfill your vow. Always remember God when He has blessed you.

6. Hannah Feared the Lord

It takes a person who fears the Lord to keep their promise. After her breakthrough she was not carried away. She expressed her awe or reverence for the

It takes a person who fears the Lord to keep their promise

Lord. She brought the child back to the house of the Lord where she had prayed during her days of desperation. There are so many things that highlight the lack of fear of God in people`s lives. This is a serious hinderance to receiving our blessings from the Lord. Make sure that you live a life that reflects reverence before God for where there`s no honour - poverty strikes.

Types of Prayers

Chapter Five

M ost Christians are not aware that there are several types of prayer discussed in God's Word. If you use one type when you should be using another type, you wont get the results you are seeking. You would be applying the wrong spiritual tool to access your needs. God intended for each of the six forms of prayer mentioned in the Bible to have different functions, as described below. Your prayer life will not be the same again after I take you through this journey of knowing the types of prayers.

1. The Prayer of Agreement

> **19 *Again I say unto you, That if two of you shall agree on earth as touching any thing that they shall ask, it shall be done for them of my Father which is in heaven.***
>
> **Matthew 18:19**

Right off the bat you can see that for the prayer of agreement to work, the people involved in the prayer have to agree! You might not know what someone else wants - what someone else is believing for - and God cannot answer your prayer for someone else against his or her will. To use the prayer of agreement, you must be sure that the person with whom you are agreeing is in line with what you are asking for. This is clear when the scripture asks in Amos 3:3, "Can two walk together, except they be agreed?"

To use the prayer of agreement, you must be sure that the person with whom you are agreeing is in line with what you are asking for.

If someone asks me to pray in agreement with them, I ask, "What specifically do you want me to pray for?" You absolutely must make sure you are in perfect agreement with their prayer request before you join with another believer in the prayer of agreement.

In Acts 12 the church was in agreement and came together to pray. This was after James had been killed by Herod Antipas who was now intend-ing to kill Peter. They gathered in prayer to counter Herod's plan. The Most High God who knows and understands the power of unity and agreement answered their prayer. He sent an angel to miraculously walk Peter out of the incarceration room! You may have to find someone to agree with you to thwart the agenda of that demonic spirit. You just might need to partner with people, particularly those who understand the pain you may be going through. I understand that we are told most of the time not to tell people what we are going through for they will laugh at us but God Himself suggests that we must agree in prayer. The prayer of agreement works. Refuse to find yourself caught up in human politics but remain in the word of God. Man's words might sound good but fail you while the Word of God might sound rough yet bring a breakthrough in your life. I see you winning as you partner in prayer with your husband against the poverty in your family.

2. The Prayer of Intercession

Intercession means you are interceding - acting in prayer on behalf of someone else. The person may be incapable of praying for himself. Perhaps he is on drugs or mentally confused by demonic doctrines. Perhaps the person is so sick he can't muster the energy to stay awake, let alone pray.

Intercession involves praying for others. It may involve praying in a general way for such things as the church or the government, or offering up more specific prayers based on your knowledge of a person's need.

15 Wherefore I also, after I heard of your faith in the Lord Jesus, and love unto all the saints, 16 Cease not to give thanks for you, making mention of you in my prayers; 17 That the God of our Lord Jesus Christ, the Father of glory, may give unto you the spirit of wisdom and revelation in the knowledge of him: 18 The

eyes of your understanding being enlightened; that ye may know what is the hope of his calling, and what the riches of the glory of his inheritance in the saints,

Ephesians 1:15-18

Here Paul makes it plain that he prayed regularly for the church at Ephesus and for the individuals there to receive these blessings. He does not set himself in agreement with anyone, so this seems to be a good example of intercessory prayer.

Likewise, in his greeting to the Philippians, he writes, *"I thank my God upon every remembrance of you, Always in every prayer of mine for you all making request with joy,"* (Philippians 1:3-4). The fact that Paul said he made requests for them suggests that this also is an example of intercessory prayer.

One of the most dangerous things in life is that we have more people against us than those who are praying for us. It is rare for people to pray for one another even in the body of Christ. People are in such desperate need that any time they have an opportunity to pray, they pray only for themselves and their children. If you discover someone who is committed to praying for you, you'd do well to respect them and find a way of honouring them. I pray that God blesses you with someone who will commit themselves to praying for your success, prosperity and breakthrough.

Personally I was blessed with a special mom who was given a burden of interceding for me day in and day out. God revealed to my biological mom that she must keep praying for me all the way. I kept advancing and am living a life of

If you discover someone who is committed to praying for you, you'd do well to respect them and find a way of honouring them.

perpetual progress as a result of her continuous prayers for me. I got a revelation of the power of intercessory prayer when my mom got terribly sick in 2014 around June. One night while I slept, I had a very disturbing vision concerning my mom and her role in my life. The vision was so meticulous to a point that I could relate every single detail of it. The gist or essence of the vision was that the enemy now had me in a tight corner because I had no one to intercede for me. I was now spiritually naked with no protection as a result of this attack on my mom's health. In the vision I saw how the enemy was playing the game and how the Lord was helping me to get on my feet.

That year as a family we went through so much and I could sense in my spirit that I was experiencing what I had seen in the vision. We thank God for His salvation. During the whole phenomenon, I remembered how Jesus had prayed for Peter.

31 And the Lord said, "Simon, Simon! Indeed, Satan has asked for you, that he may sift you

*as wheat. 32 But I have prayed for you, that
your faith should not fail; and when you have
returned to Me, strengthen your brethren."*
Luke 22:31-32(NKJV)

Saints we have an intercessor as a church. He
prays for us; He died for us; He experienced the
most excruciating pain for the sake of you and me.
Like I said, we have many imprecations or curses
against our lives. You don't have to worry. If there`s
no one to intercede for you, know that Jesus
already prayed for you and is still making intercession for you.

*20 "I do not pray for these alone, but also for
those who will believe in Me through their
word; 21 that they all may be one, as You,
Father, are in Me, and I in You; that they also
may be one in Us, that the world may believe
that You sent Me. 22 And the glory which You
gave Me I have given them, that they may
be one just as We are one: 23 I in them, and
You in Me; that they may be made perfect in
one, and that the world may know that You
have sent Me, and have loved them as You
have loved Me.*
John 17:20-23

*25 Wherefore he is able also to save them to
the uttermost that come unto God by him,
seeing he ever liveth to make intercession for
them.*
Hebrews 7:25

You are safe in God's arms so keep moving child of God.

Most of the time we think a blessing is money but I beg to differ. If God appoints people to pray for you, man you are really blessed. After my mom got sick an amazing thing

> *If there's no one to intercede for you, know that Jesus already prayed for you and is still making intercession for you.*

happened. We were to host a conference called "Refill" in a week's time. The Refill conference is our major annual event. A pastor friend who was one of our guests happened to prophesy over my mom. God was transferring the mantle of prayer to my wife. It was clear that God was on my side irrespective of the attack. From that time my wife never struggled to pray for me. I can hear her sometimes in the morning presenting my name before God. My ministry went to another level. Saints it is imperative to intercede for one another. I just love Hezekiah Walker's song that says, 'I pray for you, you pray for me, I love you, I need you to survive."

3. The Prayer of Faith

The prayer of faith, also known as petition prayer, is the prayer that most people think of when they use the term "prayer." Petition prayer is between you and God. It is you asking God for a particular outcome.

The key verse for the prayer of faith is Mark 11:24, *in which Jesus says, " Therefore I say to you, whatever things you ask when you pray, believe that you receive them, and you will have them."*

The rule to consider here is that you must believe you have received your request when you pray - not after you pray when you feel or see something. When you pray (the moment that you pray) you must believe that you have received what you asked for.

Hebrews 11:1 says, "Now faith is the substance of things hoped for, the evidence of things not seen." Your faith is substance - it is something real, something tangible. It is evidence of things you cannot see.

Notice that Mark 11:24 does not say when you will actually see the result of your prayer. It does not tell you how long it will take for that prayer result to appear. This is where many Christians get hung up.

God lives in eternity. There is no past or present for Him. As human beings we live in a realm of time and therefore we process our world in the context of time.

When you pray in faith, God immediately gives you what you prayed for—in the spirit realm. But in the natural world, due to a number of factors, it may take time for the answer to manifest itself.

God answers prayers, and He will answer your specific prayer in line with His Word, but it is your faith that brings that answer out of the spiritual world and into the physical world. How many times in Scripture does Jesus say to someone, "*According to your faith*"?

He referred to people's faith constantly. Even though it was His power that healed them, He always credited their faith with being the **catalyst**. In fact, when Jesus went to His hometown, we are told that "*He did not do many mighty works there because of their unbelief*" (Matthew 13:58). Did Jesus suddenly lose His power on that visit to Nazareth? No! His power never diminished so what changed? It was the people's lack of faith. There was no catalyst. A catalyst is a substance which increases the rate of a chemical reaction but is unchanged at the end of the reaction. Only a very small amount of catalyst is needed to increase the rate of reaction between large amounts of react-

God will not do anything against your will

ants. Faith as small as a mustard seed can move a mountain but no mountain can be moved without faith.

There is a simple spiritual explanation for this. God will not do anything against your will. God cannot violate free will. If you don't have faith to do something, He won't arbitrarily override your lack of faith. Here is some free advice for you to consider today as you read this book; Have faith in God and you won't go wrong in your life.

> ⁶ *But let him ask in faith, nothing wavering. For he that wavereth is like a wave of the sea driven with the wind and tossed. ⁷ For let not that man think that he shall receive any thing of the Lord. ⁸ A double minded man is unstable in all his ways.*
>
> **James 1:6-8**

The scripture makes it very clear. You must deal with a double mind when you want God to do something for you. Approach him with one mind and it shall be done for you. It is possible to be of one mind. Faith has a way of pleasing God. It has a force that mountains can`t resist. When God finds faith in you, He doesn`t mind changing His direction to attend to your situation. He can't resist faith. Ask the woman with the issue of blood and the woman of Canaan.

When God finds faith in you, He doesn`t mind changing His direction to attend to your situation.

> ²² *And, behold, a woman of Canaan came out of the same coasts, and cried unto him, saying, Have mercy on me, O Lord, thou son of David; my daughter is grievously vexed with a devil. ²³ But he answered her not a word. And his disciples came and besought him, saying, Send her away; for she crieth*

after us. 24 But he answered and said, I am not sent but unto the lost sheep of the house of Israel. 25 Then came she and worshipped him, saying, Lord, help me. 26 But he answered and said, It is not meet to take the children's bread, and to cast it to dogs. 27 And she said, Truth, Lord: yet the dogs eat of the crumbs which fall from their masters' table. 28 Then Jesus answered and said unto her, O woman, great is thy faith: be it unto thee even as thou wilt. And her daughter was made whole from that very hour.

Matthew 15:22-28

Child of God never say another prayer if you have no faith that the Lord is able to meet your need. It will be a waste of time as your lack of faith will cause your prayer to go unanswered. James says ask without doubting. I see you receiving from God like never before as a result of your change of strategy in prayer. You will be in a position to receive more when you have faith. Nothing in the Lord`s storeroom will be denied you if you have faith. The prayer of faith will influence your level of receiving from the Lord.

4. The Prayer of Consecration and Dedication

In the book of Luke, we see outlined the prayer of consecration and dedication.

41 And he was withdrawn from them about a stone's cast, and kneeled down, and prayed, 42 Saying, Father, if thou be willing, remove

this cup from me: nevertheless not my will, but thine, be done.

Luke 22:41-42

He was praying, in effect, "If there is any other way to do this, let's do it that way." But the key for Jesus - as it should be for us - was, "*Nevertheless not my will, but Yours, be done.*" You pray that God's will should be done when you don't know His will or you don't know if an alternative path that appears is equally "correct" or godly. In the absence of direct instructions, the prayer of consecration and dedication says you will allow God to set your direction and have the final say.

The prayer of consecration and dedication works when you have two (or more) godly alternatives before you, and you are not getting a clear sense at that time about which option God wants you to take. When the direction is unclear - but the options appear to be legitimate, righteous options - that is the perfect time to say, "Lord, if it be Your will, I'm going to go with option A."

> *Nothing in the Lord's storeroom will be denied you if you have faith.*

Believe me; He will let you know if you are taking the wrong fork in the road. I also need you to know why it is important for you to pray this type of prayer and I highlighted when this prayer is applicable. Most of the time we fail to reach our ultimate goals in life because too many options and feelings attack our lives during the time God wants to glorify us. We often opt to take the path that is most convenient to us. If you are to be great in life, don't always make decisions based on convenience. The scripture says there are two ways. One is easy, convenient and looks good. Most people are choosing to travel this convenient path. King Jesus advised that we choose the hard road for there is life at the end of it. This path looks tough and sometimes it seems like you're losing your mind along the way, but you shall enjoy the beauty that comes at the end.

> **8 Better is the end of a thing than the beginning thereof: and the patient in spirit is better than the proud in spirit.**
>
> *Ecclesiastes 7:8*

One thing you need to remember is that you have the right to choose. Life and death are in your tongue. Choose life. It's time you offered this prayer so that God`s will for your life can prevail. This time around you shall not miss your glory. The will of God comes with glory for your life. It is my firm belief, based on scriptures like 1 Corinthians 10:13, that when you offer this type of prayer you will be strengthened to stand and go through the process for you to be glorified by the Lord thereafter.

If you are to be great in life, don't always make decisions based on convenience.

5. The Prayer of Praise and Worship

In this prayer, you are not asking God to do something for you or to give you something. You are not even asking for direction or dedicating your life to whatever it is God has called you to do. Rather, you just want to praise the Lord and thank Him for His many blessings and for His mercy. You want to tell Him how much you love Him.

A good example of this type of prayer appears in the book of Luke which describes the reaction of the shepherds who had seen baby Jesus.

20 *And the shepherds returned, glorifying and praising God for all the things that they had heard and seen, as it was told unto them.*
Luke 2:20

In Luke 18:43, the blind man who was healed was described as "glorifying God." The verse also says all the people who witnessed the miracle "gave praise to God." They prayed prayers of thanksgiving. In John 11:41 Jesus thanked His Father for hearing him, referring to his previous prayer for Lazarus. In the Lord's prayer, Jesus told his disciples, *"When you pray, say: Our Father in heaven, hallowed be Your name"* (Luke 11:2 NKJV).

Paul wrote to the Philippians: *"Be anxious for nothing, but in everything by prayer and supplication, with thanksgiving, let your requests be made known to God;"* (Philippians 4:6). This reveals to us that the prayer of faith should always be interspersed with worship and praise.

You will remember that Jesus told the Samaritan woman at the well in John 4:24 that God is looking for true worshippers; the kind who worship in spirit and in truth. God is faithful in our lives so we shouldn't be struggling to worship Him for who He is. He has proven in so many ways that He loves us and He wants us to just worship Him. Wherever you are reading this book from, regardless of what you are going through, or who you are, all I want you to do is to make time, before the end of the day, to begin to praise and worship the Lord. Until you learn how to praise and worship God, you will struggle to accept yourself and that which the Lord has done for you. Child of God you are a royal priesthood. This means that you are ordained to praise and worship Him. It is an office and a duty.

Praise Him for what He has done in your life. Praise Him for protection and for His provision. Praise Him for His love. Worship Him for He is Almighty; worship Him for being our creator.

You are a royal priesthood. This means that you are ordained to praise and worship Him. It is an office and a duty.

6. The Prayer of Binding and Loosing

18 Verily I say unto you, Whatsoever ye shall bind on earth shall be bound in heaven: and whatsoever ye shall loose on earth shall be loosed in heaven. 19 Again I say unto you, That if two of you shall agree on earth as touching any thing that they shall ask, it shall

be done for them of my Father which is in heaven.

Matthew 18:18-19

There are several important nuggets in Jesus' statements here, the first being that we have authority here on Earth by virtue of our covenant rights through Jesus. The second thing we notice is the direction of the action. Things do not begin in Heaven and come to Earth, but rather the action starts here on Earth. Notice that it says, *"Whatsoever ye shall bind on earth shall be bound in heaven: and whatsoever ye shall loose on earth shall be loosed in heaven."*

Like all things in God's system, this type of prayer works only in line with God's Word and His laws. You cannot bind things willy-nilly. Binding a team to lose in the Super Bowl won't work any more than loosing someone to love you.

You can, however, bind foul spirits that are at work in people's lives or loose angelic spirits to work on your behalf in those areas where God has already promised you results. When you pray in this manner, God affirms it in Heaven and puts His seal of approval on your prayer. Binding and loosing have to be based on the authority God has granted you in Scripture, not on some desire you have.

God has provided each type of prayer for a specific purpose. Though you may use more than one at any given time, it is important to be clear about which type you are using and why. You must also be aware of its limitations. If you follow the examples in the Bible, you'll be sure to use them properly.

Conclusion

*T*hank you for taking this journey with me and for allowing me to share with you what the Lord has taught me about prayer. The desire of my heart is that you will not only learn but that you will begin to practise the *Art of Prayer*!

It takes a humble man to pray....

About the Author

Apostle N.E. Ngoveni is a born again child of God. He was born and raised in Makoxa Village in the Limpopo province of the Republic Of South Africa. His ministry began when he served as a lead worshipper and pianist in the Assemblies of God church. He is married to Pastor Alicia Ngoveni, a woman of purpose who causes him to excel in his calling. They are blessed with two children - Nyiketo and Pamela Ngoveni.

He is the President, General Overseer and Senior Pastor of Impact House Ministries with headquarters in Roodepoort, South Africa. He is a host of the program "Tell Your Story (TYS)" which is aimed at impacting the lives of many by hosting well-known, profound and influential people of our time. Annually he hosts the "Refill Conference" in Johannesburg where Kingdom people are refilled through the word. He also hosts "Kingdom Worship" which is aimed at raising an altar for God in different regions of the world to bring about spiritual upliftment.

Apostle Ngoveni is a revelatory teacher of the word of God who is zealous to nurture and pastor the gifts and callings upon people's lives. He is an apostle by grace and calling, a radiographer by profession and a teacher of the word by function. He carries an apostolic mantle that has a ground breaking unction, enabling him to break and establish new grounds. His mission is to provoke the purpose of God in humanity. This has propelled him to raise an army of sons and daughters in the Kingdom of God who have become influential in every sphere of life.

He is a sought after Conference, Radio, TV, and Crusade Speaker. He has ministered across South Africa, in Namibia, Nigeria, Zambia and many more nations.

"Your purpose carries your story, and your story carries your glory"

APOSTLE N.E NGOVENI.

www.ingramcontent.com/pod-product-compliance
Lightning Source LLC
Chambersburg PA
CBHW071826020426
42331CB00007B/1616